Forgiveness

An Act of Violence

Pastor John B. Lowe II

D0423703

John B. Lowe II

Copyright © 2018 John B. Lowe II

Pulpit to Page Publishing Co. books may be ordered through booksellers or by contacting:

Pulpit to Page Publishing Co.
Warsaw, Indiana
pulpittopage.com

ISBN: 978-1981250073
ISBN: 1981250077

Library of Congress Control Number: 2017964651

ENDORSEMENTS

Pastor John Lowe has done us all a great favor by putting into writing some tremendous insights and wisdom about the power of forgiveness. The truths in this book are life-changing, and Pastor John's style is refreshing, down-to-earth, and highly practical. This book contains powerful scriptural principles and gripping illustrations that will have you searching your own heart. I highly recommend that you read this book with an open mind and apply these transformational principles of forgiveness in your own life. Your life will be richer for it, and you will enjoy life and people much more when these truths are implemented in your life. Thank you, Pastor John, for sharing as you have with all of us.

—**Tony Cooke**, Author and Bible Teacher
Broken Arrow, Oklahoma

I have had the privilege to know Pastor John B. Lowe for well over thirty years. He has always been there for me as a self-sacrificial loyal friend who sticks closer than a brother. The subject of forgiveness that John writes about in this book is clearly evidenced in his own life, as he lives free from guilt and shame and has a clean heart in his love for God and others.

Out of all the rich grace that God gives in Jesus, I find His forgiveness is the most beautiful to see. Jesus demonstrated this grace so perfectly when in His suffering, when justice was denied Him, He prayed for our forgiveness and more than that, paid for it with His own precious blood.

On these pages John sets out how to live in this forgiveness and gives many practical ways of how to share it with others. I pray that as you read, the rich treasury of God's grace opens to your soul to heal you and enable you to share His forgiveness with others.

—**Robert Maasbach**, Pastor and Author
LifeChurch Folkestone, England

I dedicate this book to my bride of 41 years who has received, given, and lived forgiveness. My wife Debbie has a sincere desire to never allow hurts to clog her relationship with Jesus.

I also dedicate this book to my children and grandchildren, who are the arrows in my life. May they go farther in the Kingdom and be on target while quenching all the fiery darts of the enemy.

Table of Contents

Introduction 8

1 Forgiveness that Alters 11

2 The Initial Hit 25

3 Dealing with the Aftermath 34

4 Forgiveness on a National Level 48

5 They Don't Know What They Do 58

6 Saintly Revenge 66

7 Forgiveness: The Word of Faith 75

8 Home-style Forgiveness 85

9 The Nuts and Bolts 98

10 Bitterness: The Evangelism Damn ... 118

11 I Forgive Me 124

Closing Thoughts 133

For more information and resources from Pastor John B. Lowe II visit:

ihavenewlife.com

Or call / write to:
New Life Christian Church & World Outreach
744 S. 325 E.
Warsaw, Indiana 46580

(574) 269-5851

Introduction

After preaching on this subject in many settings in several nations, I've found that the phrase "Forgiveness: An Act of Violence" causes folks to recoil. We typically think violence is something to be forgiven, not something that forgiveness causes. However, forgiveness does release violence. Not on people, but on the plan of hell.

I remember hearing a study done in which crowds of people were asked on the street, "Do you believe God has a plan for your life?" I was encouraged to hear that 90 percent of the people did indeed believe that God had a plan. What's more is that God isn't the only one with a plan. The devil also has a plan for your life. That plan consists of three things: steal, kill, and destroy. John 10:10 spells it out plainly. Scripturally and practically, Satan introduces his destructive plans into our lives through a means called unforgiveness. The harboring of bitterness certainly isn't a topic for the mere sinner, but it's one that's just as pertinent to the church.

In the King James Version of the Bible, the words *forgive*, *forgave*, and *forgiveness* are used over 40 times in Matthew, Mark, and Luke. However, the book of John doesn't mention those words at all. The gospel according to Matthew was written to the Jews. The gospel of Mark was penned to the Roman Gentiles. Likewise, Luke was also written to the Gentiles. However, there is something different about the gospel according to St. John. The book of John was written to the church. Why would a book written to the church seemingly miss such a big topic? Simple! Because the church is supposed to be absolutely, beyond question, acquainted with the topic of forgiveness on every level.

The intention of this book is to explain the reasons for forgiveness and encourage the act of forgiveness. Many talk about the call of God in terms of ministry and missions. The call of God which supersedes those ventures is to forgive as we've been forgiven. You'll find three helpful review questions at the end of each chapter that you can answer in your private devotion or in small group settings. I pray that in these pages, you'd find grace and instruction to release offenses as quickly as they come.

Chapter One

Forgiveness that Alters

"If I am forgiven without being altered, forgiveness is not only damaging to me, but a sign of unmitigated weakness in God." — Oswald Chambers

The unmatched forgiveness of God is worthy of our marveling. From the beginning of the earth, God has shown His effort and desire to pardon mankind. Psalm 103:12 declares, "As far as the east is from the west, So far has He removed our transgressions from us". Explorers have located the South Pole. They've also mapped and marked the North Pole.

Interestingly enough, they haven't pinpointed, and cannot pinpoint, the East Pole or the West Pole. Why? Because they don't exist. The west continues west until you make a full circle. Likewise the east continues east until you get back to where you started. There is no end to east and west. The picture God is painting in this Psalm is one that says, "My forgiveness is unending." Our challenge is wrapping a finite brain around infinite forgiveness.

The scriptures also declare, "He will again have compassion on us, And will subdue our iniquities. You will cast all our sins into the depths of the sea." (Micah 7:19) God throws sin from Him and from us. And let me inform you... God has a good arm. Forgiven sin sinks, never again to resurface. If we would understand the true depth of His forgiveness, it would alter our lives. I know one man who has been saved and walking faithfully with the Lord for decades. His entire testimony and ministry is based on the fact that he refuses to forget just how much he has been *forgiven.*

God hasn't forgiven us like this for us to merely applaud and appreciate. No, He has done this that we might be *changed* by it. If forgiveness hasn't altered you, you've received a bit of a moral bath but not true forgiveness. Receiving God's sin-removing, conscious-cleansing forgiveness literally redirects the course of our lives so that we don't keep going back into the same snare that we had to get forgiven of in the first place. God's kind of forgiveness inspires changes, breaks cycles, and alters our future. It's impossible to forgive others without laying a foundation of just how much we ourselves have been forgiven.

Let's look at a story from the book of Luke that reinforces this truth.

"And Jesus answered and said to him, 'Simon, I have something to say to you.' So he said, 'Teacher, say it.'

"'There was a certain creditor who had two debtors. One owed five hundred denarii, and the other fifty. And when they had nothing with which to repay, he freely forgave them both. Tell Me, therefore, which of them will love him more?'

"Simon answered and said, 'I suppose the one whom he forgave more.'

"And He said to him, 'You have rightly judged.' Then He turned to the woman and said to Simon, 'Do you see this woman? I entered your house; you gave Me no water for My feet, but she has washed My feet with her tears and wiped them with the hair of her head. You gave Me no kiss, but this woman has not ceased to kiss My feet since the time I came in. You did not anoint My head with oil, but this woman has anointed My feet with fragrant oil.

"'Therefore I say to you, her sins, which are many, are forgiven, for she loved much. But to whom little is forgiven, the same loves little.'" (Luke 7:40-47)

Those who have been forgiven much, love much. Does that exempt a "cleaned-up" lifelong Christian from loving because they haven't needed much forgiveness? Absolutely not. Why? Because we've all been forgiven the same. James 2:10 says, "For whoever shall keep the whole law, and yet stumble in one point, he is guilty of all."

What does that tell us? Each one of us is guilty of every trespass. Some say, "Well, what if I haven't gone out into the drinking, drug, sex, and party life? Am I still guilty of it all?" Yes! Before Christ, we were guilty of breaking the whole law. Yet in God's redemptive nature, He saw that the forgiveness of such a massive debt would produce lovers of a heavenly kind. The fact that you've been forgiven of breaking the whole law ought to inspire you to give a whole love, nothing left out and nothing reserved.

When the grace we've received from God is *truly* internalized, it then becomes *externalized.* We switch from crying *because* of people to crying *for* people. We are no longer the victims, we are the victors.

I grew up with a sort of moral code that I

lived by. I didn't go out looking to hurt people; however, if they hurt me, it was game on. It was a revenge mentality that permeated the culture I was raised in. I had never allowed God's forgiveness which He extended to me to change me. It wasn't even a thought. Once I gave my life to Jesus, His forgiveness began deeply altering my life.

I remember an experience I had while in Bible school in Oklahoma. I was working full time, in Bible school full time, a husband and father full time, and sleeping part time. One day when I was leaving to go to Bible school, there were a couple young guys smoking pot and loitering on our porch. With a wife and young kids at home by themselves during the day, I naturally didn't want any scoundrels hanging around outside of our apartment. I confronted them and told them to find another place to go.

They left and we had no issues... until the next day. As I left for school again, they were loitering again. I sternly warned them to leave. They left. When I came back from Bible school, they were back on the porch again. As you can imagine, I wasn't happy. I went inside and changed out of my preaching clothes and changed into my fighting clothes. I went outside and found the guys in the apartment complex's communal laundry room. I proceeded to beat both of them up badly. I threw one guy over the laundry machine and really started pounding the other. As I was about to deliver a finishing punch to one of them, from his knees he screamed out at me, "I know you're a Christian, and because of you, I'll never accept Jesus!"

With those words, I was arrested by the Holy Spirit. I was crushed. I stopped in my tracks, let the man go, and walked back to our apartment. I went upstairs and laid on my face and wept before the Lord. I felt so sorry for allowing my old self back into the picture. I prayed and prayed, asking God to help reverse what I had done. I prayed for the guys I had beat up and prayed for God to fix the situation.

In the midst of the prayer, I heard God say to me, "You fix it." I was wanting someone else to repair the damage. God wanted me to restore the situation. He told me to finish folding the guys' laundry, walk it over to their apartment, repent, and ask them to forgive me. That alone is quite a humbling act. Yet He didn't stop there. He said, "When you ask him to forgive you, I want you to give him a kiss on the cheek."

From there I got up, went to the laundry

room, and finished folding their laundry. I took the basket to their apartment and knocked on the door. The guy opened the door, but only as much as the chain lock would allow. They were both naturally quite fearful, thinking that I was showing up for another tango.

I said, "I'm here to tell you I'm sorry for the way I acted earlier. Will you forgive me?" The guy was absolutely stunned. His buddy stood behind him with a baseball bat, quite skeptical. Shocked and caught off guard, he responded, "Yeah... I forgive you."

I started to turn around to walk away. The Holy Spirit stopped me and said, "You're forgetting something." I turned around, humbled and a bit reluctant, and said, "God told me I have to kiss you on the cheek." In the background, his buddy yelled, "Don't

do it, man. He is gonna sucker punch you."
I said, "I won't hit you. I promise. God told
me I have to do this, so if you won't let me,
I'll stand out here on the porch all night if I
have to." At that point, the man finally
peaked his head out of the door just enough
for me to kiss him on the cheek. I went
home with a new found humility.

Later that evening, the man who received
the kiss on the cheek came over to our
apartment and said, "I've never in my life
had anyone ask me for forgiveness." He was
awestruck and moved. We shared and
ministered the gospel to him and he gave
his life to Jesus that night.

Not many days after the event, his buddy
who didn't come over to talk with us was
out with a group playing chicken on the
roads. He was driving 65 on the wrong side

of the road and collided head on with an oncoming car, killing him instantly. The guy we led to the Lord would have been with him, had he not gotten saved that night.

Forgiveness released us both. It released me from destroying a man's chance at heaven. It released the young man from his sins. Forgiveness, in its violent mercy, released us both from bitterness and the opportunity to harbor a grudge. It freed the man and allowed him to be saved and protected from an early death.

When forgiveness alters us, it causes us to do things that we would have otherwise never done. It brings about a humility and an understanding of our need to experience continual reconciliation with God and with our fellow man.

Review Questions:

In what specific ways has *receiving* forgiveness altered and changed you?

_____

_____

_____

_____

_____

_____

_____

_____

_____

In what areas of your life do you need to allow forgiveness to bring about continued change?

_____

_____

_____

_____

_____

_____

_____

_____

_____

As mentioned in the chapter, how can you *internalize* God's truth and then *externalize* it?

_____

_____

_____

_____

_____

_____

_____

_____

Chapter Two

The Initial Hit

"So Jesus answered and said to them, "Have faith in God. For assuredly, I say to you, whoever says to this mountain, 'Be removed and be cast into the sea,' and does not doubt in his heart, but believes that those things he says will be done, he will have whatever he says. Therefore I say to you, whatever things you ask when you pray, believe that you receive them, and you will have them.

And whenever you stand praying, if you have anything against anyone, forgive him, that your Father in heaven may also forgive you your trespasses. But if you do not forgive, neither will your Father in heaven forgive your trespasses." (Mark 11:22-26)

I began ministry in the former Soviet Union in the early 90's. I've done ministry many times near Chernobyl, the famous location of the massive nuclear meltdown. I've found it interesting in researching that in the *initial* Chernobyl meltdown, two people died. Such a massive, well circulated event, yet only two died initially. Now, don't get me wrong — one death is too many. But how did the news of the explosion reach such worldwide hype with only two dying initially? Because it wasn't the initial hit that did the most damage. Rather, it was the aftermath that did. In fact, another 29 died in hospitals over the course of the few days following. But it doesn't end there. A 2011 article by Roger Highfield states, "Two decades ago, John Gittus of the Royal Academy of Engineering told the UK government there could eventually be around 10,000 fatalities.

Today, some – notably environmental groups – put the death toll well into six figures."

The aftermath is harder to quantify but absolutely dwarfs the size of the initial impact. Whether it was radiation in the air, contaminated water, or exposure to harmful chemicals, the effects of the explosion continued to live on, adding to the death toll.

In our lives, the initial damage from an offense is painful. People wound us, hurt us, hurt our family, sin against us, and offend us. You don't have to live long to realize that people are capable of ruffling our feathers, so to speak. Yet it's imperative that we understand that the damage done in the initial impact is small compared to the long term possibilities if the hit isn't dealt with effectively. The initial offense doesn't hurt us as much as the aftermath. Someone could steal a moment from you, and they will — but refuse to allow them to steal weeks, months, years, or even a lifetime. Some think that harboring an offense like a pet is a sign of strength, and that releasing an offense is somehow weak. I've got news for you; it takes more strength to forgive than to refuse to forgive. I remember hearing a story about an insane initial hit that could have become a mess of radioactive bitterness in the person's life, but fortunately, it was dealt with properly.

Oprah actually covered the story. A young mom had been with a horrendous man. The relationship was so poisonous that things escalated to abusive levels. One day, the man went on an absolute tear. He beat her up, raped her, shot her, and left her for dead with her son present. He took off and later was caught, arrested, and rightfully thrown in prison.

The precious lady fell into a coma and stayed that way for some time. Finally, she snapped out of the coma. The words that came out of her mouth *immediately* upon exiting the coma were, "I forgive him." Wow! Starting with those words will set the course straight from the beginning. From there, she became healthy enough to leave the hospital. She then started going to the prison every single week to tell him, "I forgive you, I love you, God has a plan for you." Simple words? Yes. But definitely words that can melt the heart of the person who is guilty of the offense. Eventually through this persistence, she brought the man to the saving knowledge of Jesus Christ and had a great impact on his life. She communicated this entire story and the details on camera while being interview by Oprah.

At this point in the interview, the cameras turned to the lady's son who was also part of the segment. Oprah inquired to him, "Have you forgiven?" He stated plainly, "No, I have not." Oprah said, "You know that you need to." I thought to myself, "Go get em, O!"

The man began shaking and crying profusely. Millions were watching. His mom was next to him, still working through physical issues and slow speech from the event. The pressure was on. He finally looked to the man who had done this heinous act and said, "I forgive you." There wasn't a dry eye in the house, including my own. Why? Because I know the healing that was just brought into that man's life. To summarize the entire event, the lady stated, "He took one night of my life and I refuse to give him another second."

I tell you with complete confidence that the initial hit doesn't have to become a lifetime event!

Sources Cited

Highfield, Roger. "25 Years after Chernobyl, We Don't Know How Many Died." *New Scientist*, 21 Apr. 2011, newscientist.com/article/dn20403-25-years-after-chernobyl-we-dont-know-how-many-died/

Review Questions:

What has been the toughest "initial hit" that you've dealt with in your life?

_____

_____

_____

_____

_____

_____

_____

_____

How can you prevent that initial hit from becoming a lifetime event?

_____

_____

_____

_____

_____

_____

_____

_____

What steps can you take to prevent the

hurt(s) from occurring again?

_____

_____

_____

_____

_____

_____

_____

_____

_____

Chapter Three

Dealing with the Aftermath

"I distinctly remember forgetting that." —
Clara Barton

In the same way that a geiger counter detects radiation, the Holy Spirit detects the toxic aftermath of an event in our heart and makes it known. Why? So we can be aware and respond accordingly. In terms of an offense — the aftermath seems to always far outweigh the initial punch. In fact, we can carry severe, heavy aftermath that all started with a microscopic, tiny offense.

I know a pastor who stood up in the middle

of praise and worship with an inspired word from God to give to the congregation. When he stood up to share, the worship leader stopped him and said, "No, we have more songs." Sorry, God is okay with interrupting your songs when He wants to speak and move. Unfortunately, the worship leader became hurt and offended that he was cut short. The pastor obviously had no foul intentions; he simply wanted to obey. However, the devil will take a minor offense and begin to play it over in your mind. "The pastor doesn't value your time and gifting. He doesn't understand the work you put into that song and now you can't even perform it. He is jealous of your gifting. You'd be happier at another church. Current leadership isn't spiritual enough for you..." And just like that, a mole hill becomes a mountain made of lies. At all cost, at all times, refuse offense.

QUARANTINE YOUR OFFENSE

Following a hurt, we typically want to talk to others about it, and often in the wrong spirit. Offense can be transmitted. When we spew our offense to others, we spread the illness of offense to them. When this happens, people who were once blind to the situation now become aware and hurt, as well.

Here's a tip: don't involve people in the conflict if they don't *need* to be involved in the conflict. Only involve those who are directly involved and wise counselors or leaders who can help. In the medical field, we quarantine the sick. It's not for the sake of the sick. They're sick regardless. It's for the sake of those around them. Quarantine your offense, lest it hop into someone else's heart. We've all been in settings where someone is sharing their story and you instantly become offended at the person who hurt them. We sympathetically take on a bitter posture, if we aren't careful. It's best to prevent the entire contagion by quarantining your hurt and dealing with it properly and privately.

"And be kind to one another, tenderhearted, forgiving one another, even as God in Christ forgave you." (Ephesians 4:32) Here's the question: how were you forgiven? The answer: totally and completely. God did not go to others with your sin which was against Him. He took it upon Himself, dealt with it properly, and extended mercy when you didn't deserve it. If we call ourselves Christians, we ought to look at our standard for forgiveness. It isn't how the world forgives. Our standard isn't how we happen to feel that day. Our standard is the total and complete forgiveness of Christ.

Right after the Chernobyl explosion, an immediate quarantine effort took place. To stop the radiation from spreading, pilots flew helicopters over Chernobyl to pour mass amounts of lead and concrete over the plant. Some of those men died in days, but all of the pilots died within two weeks of the event due to radioactive poisoning. They gave their lives to prevent the spread of something dangerous. They knew it would be worth it to sacrifice themselves to see to it that more lives are saved. If spreading toxic radiation is worth sacrificing for on a natural level, how much more is it worth sacrificing for on a spiritual level? We must be willing to give our lives away to this thing called Christianity to see to it that our hearts stay soft and offense doesn't spread.

Clara Barton, the founder of the American

Red Cross, was reminded one day of a nasty thing that someone had done to her in the year prior. But she acted like she had never even heard of the incident. "Don't you remember it?" her friend asked. "No," came Barton's reply, "I distinctly remember forgetting it."

INSTANT REPLAY

God has forgiven and intentionally forgotten our sin. The sea of forgetfulness is the container of our sin, not God's mind. Just like God chose to forget, we also make the choice to forget. Rehearsing offense after it occurs is a tool of the devil.

"Then Peter came to Him and said, 'Lord, how often shall my brother sin against me, and I forgive him? Up to seven times?' Jesus said to him, 'I do not say to you, up to seven times, but up to seventy times seven.'"

(Matthew 18:21-22)

In the book of Amos, Amos mentioned the number 3 eight different times, in terms of forgiveness. In Matthew 18, Peter upped the commitment to a potential 7 opportunities for forgiveness in a day. Jesus Christ upped the ante all together and proposed 7 X 70 per day. In other words, as many times as offense comes, you release it. Now, I'm not the smartest guy in the bunch, but I can do the math. Seventy times seven is 490. And if someone offends me that many times in a single day, I am smart enough to leave the room. However, I believe what Jesus was dealing with wasn't just the physical offense, but the replaying of it in the mind. A person could offend you deeply one time. The devil can show up and replay that offense 490 times in a day minimum and you have to refuse the offense each time.

For example, I remember being at a friend's house watching the NFL as a kid in the 60's. The star running back sprinted into the end zone and scored a touchdown. We all cheered and celebrated. Seconds later, an instant replay hits the screen showing the touchdown again. My friend and I watched calmly while his dad went ballistic, hopped out of his seat and shouted, "Oh, my goodness! Did you see that?! He just scored another touchdown within seconds of the last one! Wow!" Needless to say, instant replay was a brand new invention in the 60's, and my buddy's dad wasn't yet acquainted. My friend went on to inform his pops about the new technology.

Much like the newfound "instant replay" for my friend's dad, Satan can bring the replay of an offense to us over and over and it can be just as real and impactful as the original attack.

I remember talking to a group of young Bible school students going into ministry in England. I shared specifically on offense and how going into ministry isn't nearly as important or impressive as *staying* in the ministry. It's like getting married. Saying vows is easy. Really easy. It's the lifelong proposition of becoming ONE that is work. The key ingredient for longevity in the ministry, or any other massive commitment for that matter, is keeping your heart out of the bondage of bitterness. As a leader, you'll have opportunity to be hurt more than anyone. People will approach you and say, "you hurt me" or "you offended me." If we aren't careful, we can get offended that they are offended. We can get hurt that they're hurt. We can get offended that folks judge our action instead of our motive. We can get hurt that people might see our shortcomings instead of our hidden sacrifice. Even while writing this, it's easy to justify and see the logical side of being bitter... and herein lies the issue. If Satan can get you to rationalize unforgiveness, you will harbor pain and could potentially pass it on for years to come. You'll spread it when you're called to quarantine it.

The Bible isn't a list of "don'ts"; it's a book of "do's". The scriptures only restrict the actions that derail your life. The Bible doesn't restrict you; it frees you. Nothing introduces more liberty into your life than the beauty of a pure heart and clean conscience before God and man.

At the end of His life, Jesus cried out, "Father forgive them." I believe this declaration released Him from the cross. If

He hadn't released that, He would have stayed nailed to it. He Himself said, "It is proper for us to do this to fulfill all righteousness." (Matthew 3:15 NIV) He had a "to-do" list that needed to be complete in order for His sufferings to be fulfilled and for His life to be committed to His Father. People won't release that which they harbor. As a result, they're nailed to their own personal cross. We become unable to move into the next stage of life with God when we nail ourselves to an unnecessary cross called unforgiveness.

Christ not only modeled this life, but He taught this life. In Luke 6:46, Jesus said, "Why do you call me, 'Lord, Lord,' and do not do what I say?"(NIV) In context, the whole chapter is about forgiveness. Calling on His name means we should do what He does... and what does He do? He forgives.

Forgiveness is one of the greatest things you'll ever enjoy. When I was forgiven, I went from darkness to light. From a child of Lucifer to a child of God. God didn't design you to walk in self pity. He wants to point to you and display you as someone who has experienced and given the power of forgiveness. Only by this revelation can we begin to shake off the aftermath of the offense, quarantine it properly, and uproot it for good!

Review Questions:

What are some practical steps to take for quarantining an offense and containing the damage?

_____

_____

_____

_____

_____

_____

_____

_____

_____

Have you ever dealt with "instant replay" from a hurt? How have you dealt with it? How should you deal with it?

_____

_____

_____

_____

_____

_____

_____

_____

What would be the outcome of refusing to quarantine an explosive happening in your life?

_____

_____

_____

_____

_____

_____

_____

_____

_____

Chapter Four

Forgiveness on a National Level

"With malice toward none, with charity for all, with firmness in the right as God gives us to see the right, let us strive on to finish the work we are in, to bind up the nation's wounds, to care for him who shall have borne the battle and for his widow and his orphan, to do all which may achieve and cherish a just and lasting peace among ourselves and with all nations." —Abraham Lincoln

I was recently at a community gathering in town to promote prayer for our nation. At the gathering, I recited the Gettysburg address prayer. The history of the address is really quite interesting. The day it was delivered, someone took most of Abraham Lincoln's talking time, so Lincoln quickly rewrote it and was sure to keep the essentials and "must shares."

What was the heart of Lincoln's message? Forgiveness toward *all* and malice toward *none*. This simple theme brought healing and reconciliation to a nation that was divided from a war that caused a greater death toll than any other in the history of the country to this day. I believe that a blessing has been attached to the USA for maintaining a national posture of *forgiveness*. Consider this: during WWI and WWII, we could have taken part of Europe permanently. Yet forgiveness was extended toward all and malice toward none. We could have violated terms of surrender toward Japan, yet we maintain protection for them to this day. Why? Because of forgiveness toward all and malice toward none. During Vietnam, the Korean War, and even modern wars like Iraq, we could have jumped into a tangled mess of national bitterness that increased the death toll and decreased the peace and tranquility. Wars are never pretty. In fact, they're ruthless. However, historically as a government, the United States has desired the best for the nations of the world — displaying this heart through unmatched aid and generosity. This is particularly displayed when aid to threatening nations is extended. Forgiveness toward all and malice toward none is a posture that has blessed and kept this country. The scriptures declare, "Blessed is the nation whose God is the Lord, The people He has chosen as His own inheritance." (Psalm 32:12)

Our international quarrels and attacks aren't inspired by a mere plot of man, but a plot of the devil. Ephesians 6 speaks about our true battle being one that isn't flesh and blood, but instead a spiritual battle. We as a nation have to deal with the devil, so to speak. It's like when you were a kid trying to hit your older brother. As hard as you tried, you couldn't reach him because there was this invisible force holding you back. What was that force? His hand on your head keeping a frustrating distance between you and him. The issue was a hand on your head holding you back. The issue isn't people offending you. The issue is the demonic force behind it trying to pour salt on the wound and increase the offense exponentially. We know that unforgiveness is very normal on an individual basis, yet we often don't consider the national ramifications of it. Our job isn't to merely defend our country from human threats both domestic and abroad, but to deal with spiritual ones.

I knew a grandfather who was married to his wife for 48 years and they had 12 kids together. He absolutely didn't have a clue how to treat his wife. After decades of marriage, she finally left him. As a result, the devil stole 48 years of covenant. Satan isn't just interested in tearing apart individuals through hard hearts; he also wants to tear apart governments, nations, and whole societies. Yet, we have to recognize that he is the snake in the grass who is behind this whole thing.

God dealt with the devil in Genesis after the fall of man. He addressed Adam, then Eve, and finally he went right down the line and confronted Satan. "So the Lord God said to the serpent: Because you have done this, you are cursed more than all cattle, and more than every beast of the field; on your belly you shall go, and you shall eat dust all the days of your life." (Genesis 3:14) God went down the line and then dealt with the devil. After that, He judged the people who yielded to Him.

It's not just a matter of shutting doors to the devil. It's eliminating the small cracks that he can jump through. Like a rat, he can get through a hole that's smaller than you can even imagine. Just like individuals can't afford compromise, our nation cannot afford compromise.

WHEN GOD DEALS WITH A NATION
Remember God's continual conversations with Israel in the Old Testament? Notice,

they were conversations with Israel... a nation. Not just individuals. The standard was remarkably strict. The rules were clear. The covenant contained the law of sin and death. God Himself said, "The soul who sins shall die." (Ezekiel 18:20) In those days, God dealt harshly with sin — because a sufficient sacrifice hadn't yet been offered, God could not separate people from sin. That was a problem, considering sin separated people from God. It was a twisted cycle. Now though, God separates people from sin so people can be one with God. How did such reconciliation come about? One word: forgiveness. The cancelling of un-payable debt.

Why did God inspire so many books in the Old Testament warning against the perils of sin and harping on such harsh topics? I believe because it was firstly a call to repentance to the people of that day. And secondly, it gave you and me a glimpse of the punishment that we miss. The greater the punishment that we miss, the greater the gratitude we have because we missed it. Dodging a slap on the wrist is easy to brush off. Dodging death, hell, and the grave causes eternal gratitude.

It's very simple: as a nation and as unique individuals and families, forgiveness is here to alter us, not excuse us. We don't plan to sin, counting on grace. We plan to live righteously — counting on grace. The goodness of God doesn't fuel sin, but draws us to Him. Many today in our nation are looking for a "feel good message." Our feel good message is forgiveness — receiving it and releasing it violently. I'm all for seeker friendly, as long as seeker friendly means seeking God, the one who forgave us and inspires us to do the exact same.

Review Questions:

What specific areas of a society are affected when tenderness is the dominant posture?

_____

_____

_____

_____

_____

_____

_____

_____

How can a nation continue to preserve godly precepts in its core?

_____

_____

_____

_____

_____

_____

_____

_____

_____

What can you do to maintain a national level forgiveness in the place God has called you?

_____

_____

_____

_____

_____

_____

_____

_____

_____

Chapter Five

They Don't Know What they do

"Then Jesus said, "Father, forgive them, for they do not know what they do." (Luke 23:34)

Really? They didn't know what they were doing? Reading verses like that challenge our logic. Christ's sufferings at the hands of the Kingdom of Darkness seemed pretty intentional to a well reasoned mind. The scourged back, nails in the hands and feet, and a spear through the side all seem to point to well planned, strategized, and intentional crucifixion. Yet somehow Jesus says, "They do not know what they do."

When we maintain a posture such as Christ's, folks say "That's a denial strategy used so you can attempt to believe the best about people." No, it isn't denial. It's the ability to see into someone's blindness. In Christ's case, the Romans knew the process of crucifixion and execution well. However, they didn't know the ramification of this particular death. They didn't have the revelation that this was God in the flesh, not until forgiveness was released and the soldier cried out, "Surely he was the Son of God!" (Matthew 27:54 NIV) How many people will recognize Jesus as Lord when they're forgiven in the midst of being guilty of heinous offense?

Jesus understood the "why" behind the soldiers' actions. For most of them, it was just a day at work, fulfilling the obligations of the higher ups. He wasn't in denial. He simply recognized that the "why" behind their offense was far less powerful than the "why" behind His forgiveness. In your life, be quick to understand the "why." Don't lose sight of what others lose sight of. Remember that those who sin against you don't know what they do, even if it feels and seems intentional and planned.

Many people refuse to forgive because the offender didn't apologize or ask for forgiveness. When Christ hung on the cross, did the anyone seek forgiveness? Of course not! The person who hurt you should apologize. But if they don't, don't stay hurt. Their apology shouldn't trigger your forgiveness. The moment the offense takes place should trigger your forgiveness. Life will hit you repeatedly with offense, shock, hurt, and drama. Your mandate is to stay soft and continue in sync with God. I remember hearing in a Rocky movie, "It's not about how hard you hit. It's about how hard you can get hit and still keep moving forward." As Christians, we are not exempt from pain and trouble. Jesus promised it. What's more, we are even more susceptible to the grace we need to move forward in the midst of the pain and trouble!

Some of the deepest wounds come from those we know best. The sting of a stranger offending you typically doesn't run as deep as the sting of a friend or family member hurting you. Yet despite this, arrows flying at you from friends or family is no reason or justification to stay offended and hurt. Forgiveness is an absolute act of violence against the aftermath of offense. It's a violent attack against the plan of Satan to bind you to bitterness. Many understand this truth yet say, "I know this is true, but I simply cannot forgive." My response? You're right!!! You cannot forgive. That's why the strength to forgive only comes from the One who commissioned us to do it! Forgiving alone is impossible. The painful process of ripping out bitterness is a task that must be done in coordination with the Holy Ghost — it's never a solo task.

"You are of God, little children, and have overcome them, because He who is in you is greater than he who is in the world." (1 John 4:4) When you draw from His grace, your "I can't" becomes an "I can!"

Believers who reject adherence to these principles find themselves in a world of turmoil. Why? Because God won't share space inside of you with bitterness. God is saying, "Forgive." Offense is screaming,

"Stay bitter." Thus, a nasty wrestling match is happening internally between your spirit and your flesh. Have you ever eaten a combination of foods that just don't mix well in your stomach? Taking in God's truth on forgiveness while feeding on thoughts about bitterness creates a mixture that won't sit right in your spirit. Jump headfirst into the short term pain of releasing hurt in order to stop the long term turmoil of harboring it. Be willing to declare toward God, "God, I forgive them and ask you to forgive them, for they don't know what they're doing." Say it by faith! Remember the "why" behind the offense. Profess that you can't forgive in your own strength. Decide to end the wrestling match.

Review Questions:

Are you willing to say, "they don't know what they do" when speaking of people who have hurt you in what seemed like a very intentional way?

_____

_____

_____

_____

_____

_____

_____

_____

_____

What are the harmful effects of a long term wrestling match between conviction and compromise?

_____

_____

_____

_____

_____

_____

_____

_____

_____

Does demanding an apology come from a place of true forgiveness? Explain your reasoning below:

_____

_____

_____

_____

_____

_____

_____

_____

_____

Chapter Six

Saintly Revenge

"When forgiveness puts you on top as the benefactor, the generous one, the giver of freedom and dignity, be careful - it could be sweet, saintly revenge." —David Ausburger

Gd doesn't forgive because He is superior... even though He is. He forgives because He is love. When extending forgiveness to us, He isn't relishing in some sick joy of feeling superior because He is being asked for mercy. If we aren't careful, we will duplicate God's model of forgiveness, which is noble, but we forget to model His heart in forgiveness. After a heated exchange or intense offense, it's tempting to look at the person who is asking for forgiveness and feel a sense of superiority. We can allow pride to take over our attitudes and mentalities. When we declare, "I forgive you," it isn't done with humility, but instead arrogance. It can become a phrase of "saintly revenge" — repaying the person and proving that you're right and they are wrong. However, when we take that sort of attitude, we are indeed still in the wrong. It is more important to be godly than to be right.

I remember once having a confrontation with a person before a church service. We could go back and forth about who was in the right and who was in the wrong. Nevertheless, we had communion that morning and I was to take the pulpit and preach. I didn't want to approach either in an unworthy manner and wanted to reconcile with this individual. I pulled them aside and asked, "Will you forgive me?"

Their response? "Yes. I forgive you." Sounds great on paper; however, their tone dripped with saintly revenge and an arrogance that said, "About time you admit that I'm right." Giving forgiveness isn't a display of your power or your position; instead, it's a display of your love.

Folks will attempt to hurt you, talk about you, and spread all sorts of injustice behind your back. When you have the chance to release such hurts, it should never be in a spirit of arrogance or saintly revenge.

THE PLACE OF GOD

The life of Joseph in general is a *workable definition* of forgiveness. Whether it was being the victim of his brothers' envy, sold into slavery, misrepresented, or thrown into prison, Joseph had chance after chance to be bitter. Despite all of this, Joseph stayed soft toward God and kept his integrity. As a result, no matter the situation or surroundings, Joseph continually prospered and got promoted. God will elevate those who live in a constant state of forgiveness.

Joseph's brothers eventually came to him to plead for forgiveness. Joseph had an interesting response. Genesis 50:19 says this, "Joseph said to them, 'Do not be afraid, for am I in the place of God?'" In other words, Joseph was not in the place of God to *punish* them. However, he *was* in the place of God to *forgive* them. Joseph was in the *place of God* — not as a power seat to look down upon the pathetic scoundrels who begged for forgiveness. He wasn't in the place of God because he was basically the vice president of the nation. He was in the place of God because he maintained a heart that cried, "I am *free* from this offense."

Folks, we stand in the place of God every time we release offense. We are made in His image and likeness, according to Genesis 1:26. When Satan wanted to lie to the first couple Adam and Eve, he said, "When you eat the fruit, you'll be like God." That was the lie and the deception — that they'd be "like God." What they didn't realize was that they already were! Don't let the devil convince you that you don't have something that you already possess. (I strongly suggest reading Genesis — chapters 37-50)

PANDORA'S BOX

"For where envying and strife is, there is confusion and every evil work." (James 3:16)

Envy and strife are like opening Pandora's

box, so to speak. Offense can create so much strife in relationships. Strife can create so much other garbage that God didn't ordain. All of the sudden, when we allow strife, everything else seems to go haywire. When we look at people, we have to look through the blood, not the flesh. **Don't look to people to see Jesus. Look to Jesus to see people.**

Samson figured out that allowing sin into his life, a hailstorm of trouble followed. He was bound, blinded, and labored at the grinding wheel before closing out his life with a final victory through repentance. We don't have to go through the trouble that Samson went through. Sin binds you, blinds you, and grinds you. Righteousness offers peace, strength, and blessing!

For me personally, I grew up with my own

code of ethics that I lived by. I didn't want to hurt people, but if they hurt me, I could hurt them back without thinking twice about it. I saw people according to the flesh. If they did what I thought was unacceptable according to John B. Lowe's code of ethics, then I had the right to harbor anything against them and treat them accordingly. This is no way to live. We aren't creating our own code of ethics. We aren't forgiving only when it benefits us personally and makes us look superior and mighty, giving us a sense of saintly revenge. No, we stand in the place of God — privileged to represent Him on this earth.

Review Questions:

List a few descriptions of a relationship that is offense proof and strife proof:

_____

_____

_____

_____

_____

_____

_____

_____

_____

In what ways do you, as a person in the earth, stand in the place of God?

_____

_____

_____

_____

_____

_____

_____

_____

What are the root causes of someone who is in "saintly revenge" and how can they uproot them?

_____

_____

_____

_____

_____

_____

_____

_____

_____

Chapter Seven

Forgiveness:
The Word of Faith

"For in Christ Jesus neither circumcision nor uncircumcision avails anything, but **faith working through love**." (Galatians 5:6 emphasis added)

T he word of faith movement historically is known for finances and healing. Those two categories are trademarks of the movement — believing God for health and wealth. Mark 11 presents the core of the word of faith message.

"So Jesus answered and said to them, Have faith in God. For assuredly, I say to you, whoever says to this mountain, 'Be removed and be cast into the sea,' and does not doubt in his heart, but believes that those things he says will be done, he will have whatever he says. Therefore I say to you, whatever things you ask when you pray, believe that you receive them, and you will have them." (Mark 11:22-23)

For so long, we have pounded the message that we ought to "believe that we receive" healing, finances, miracles, and so forth — and rightfully so, I might add! However, let's not forget the law of context in dealing with scriptures. Just after giving the teaching about faith to receive, Jesus brings up an issue that goes right along with the faith message.

"And whenever you stand praying, if you have anything against anyone, forgive him, that your Father in heaven may also forgive you your trespasses. But if you do not forgive, neither will your Father in heaven forgive your trespasses." (Mark 11:24-26)

This chapter deals with faith and receiving along with *forgiveness*. Faith and forgiveness go hand in hand. It requires great faith to *receive* forgiveness and it requires great faith to *release* forgiveness. No doubt, it takes faith to forgive. In fact, many times you don't *feel* it at all. Let your faith be the determining factor, not your feelings.

"Examine yourselves *as to* whether you are in the faith. Test yourselves..." (2 Corinthians 13:5)

Forgiveness is a faith test without question. Examining ourselves only to find a bitter heart reveals that we aren't really in the faith. Faith expresses itself through forgiveness. Faith expresses itself through love. Galatians 5:6 says, "For in Christ Jesus neither circumcision nor uncircumcision avails anything, but **faith working through love.**" (emphasis added)

Don't talk to me about believing God for a car if you aren't believing God to forgive. All too often, people push for stuff, but not for a clean heart. They will push for miracles, but not push to release offense. We want faith to receive deliverance, but what about the *forgiveness* that releases deliverance?

As mentioned earlier, we have to be willing to forget our feelings in order to forgive. It might be painful yet worth it. If feelings become our master, forgiveness won't come easy. Your feelings will fight you tooth and nail in an attempt to stay hard.

I was once preaching on righteousness. I shared in depth on coming back to right standing with God and so forth. In the middle of the message, a lady bellowed out a painful scream. It was obvious and loud. Why did she scream? She was in pain. What was the pain? The brief pain of having to forgive herself. Right in the midst of the word being preached, she finally agreed with God and found herself judged according to Christ, not her past sin. She released herself from who she was and what she had done. She was completely delivered.

SCALING DOWN THE PAIN

"For our light affliction, which is but for a moment, is working for us a far more exceeding and eternal weight of glory..." 2

Corinthians 4:17)

What was the "light affliction" that Paul was referring to in this passage? Beatings, persecution, being shipwrecked, and more. He counted big problems as light afflictions. He didn't make mountains out of molehills; he made mountains into molehills. I believe that doing so keeps you pure in heart and moves you past offense. When we judge a situation as "light affliction" and truly minor, we're able to shake it off more quickly and effectively.

"...while we do not look at the things which are seen, but at the things which are not seen. For the things which are seen *are* temporary, but the things which *are* not seen are eternal." (2 Corinthians 4:18)

Focus on that which is eternal, not temporal.

Forgiveness is an eternal act. In fact, you'll enjoy the benefit of it forever. When we become short-sighted, we tend to focus on the temporary, earthly, here-and-now sort of things. Doing so sets us up for failure. We focus on temporary things and get hurt by temporary things instead of being healed and mended by eternal truths. When we are hurt, we tend to draw back. I believe "unforgiveness" can be described as "ungiving." In that state, we struggle to give a smile. We struggle to give an act of kindness. Unforgiveness closes your hand to God and the people around you. This is the polar opposite of the will of God.

"Blessed be the God and Father of our Lord Jesus Christ, the Father of mercies and God of all comfort, who comforts us in all our tribulation, **that we may be able to comfort those who are in any trouble, with the**

comfort with which we ourselves are comforted by God." (2 Corinthians 1:3-4 emphasis added)

We have freely received the help of God, thus we ought to freely give the help of God. Living with closed hands is no way to live, yet harboring unforgiveness signs you up for it.

I know of elders who have been in fist fights in the church parking lot after frustrating board meetings. Imagine that: those who are commissioned to look after the church find themselves so embittered and offended that they are willing to throw away their integrity in order to defend their honor.

The word of faith movement has taken many shapes and forms over the years. No matter the form it takes, it must continue to always take the form of *forgiveness*. Faith to move mountains isn't impressive until it's moving your own heart to a place of forgiveness and freedom from offense. Your feelings might not agree, but the Word does.

Review Questions:

Have you been guilty of focusing stuff rather than Him?

_____

_____

_____

_____

_____

_____

_____

_____

_____

How could the "word of faith" movement benefit from focusing on forgiveness?

_____

_____

_____

_____

_____

_____

_____

_____

_____

What does "faith to forgive" look like in our
daily lives?

_____

_____

_____

_____

_____

_____

_____

_____

_____

Chapter Eight

Home-style Forgiveness

"And above all things have fervent love for one another, for love will cover a multitude of sins." (1 Peter 4:8)

In the book of Nehemiah, God commissioned His people to rebuild the wall with a hammer in one hand and a sword in the other. The men were responsible for defending their homes and families and nation with the sword while, at the same time, repairing that which was broken. The same is true for us to this day. We fight battles on many fronts while rebuilding and shaping our lives. There is something interesting in addition to the sword and the hammer. God also commissioned the men to rebuild the part of the wall that was nearest to their own homes. Nehemiah chapter 4 describes this. Why? Firstly and most practically, it's a quick commute to work. It's efficient and effective. Secondly and most importantly, you'll care more for the stuff that's near your own house.

In life, you don't just need the tools to build your home, but the sword of the Word to keep it pure and fend off attacks. Not only that, you're called to care deeply and invest time in the stuff that's nearest your home. Your home must be the safe haven for your family. This only happens through investment and commitment to keep hearts pure and motives right.

OUR STORY

In my own home, the first few years were a lovely mess of hell on earth. Unlike Nehemiah and the gang, I worked hard at tearing down my marriage. My wife Debbie and I met in a strip joint. She was stripping and traveling and wrapped up in a bad gang of people. I was a hot-headed jerk who had a shot at professional football. Debbie had just discovered that the man she had been with for a long time was married. Devastated, she said to her friend, "The next guy who walks through that door is mine." Who was the next guy? Me. She came over and kissed me. We got married four weeks later.

Without having any clue about how to do marriage, forgiveness, and communication, life became terrible quickly. After three years, Debbie and I were one signature away from divorce. We didn't get along, adultery was taking place on both sides, and hardness of heart had more than set in. Easter Sunday was approaching and Debbie pleaded with me to go to church. I said, "I'll go with you under one condition: after church is over, you leave and never come back." I went to church literally to get rid of my wife. That Easter Sunday, I answered the altar call and got saved. Our lives began to change and we decided that if we were going to call ourselves Christians, then we'd act like Christians and sell out.

We began praying and attending church every single time the doors were open. We moved from West Virginia to Michigan for one reason and one reason only: to attend Agape Christian Center — a charismatic gathering where the Holy Ghost was active and people *actually* acted like they wanted to be there! It was the first time we'd seen a church where people were loving, kind, and "huggy." We loved serving and growing there.

Deb and I had been saved a few months, and we were getting better. We had a big fight one day. I was unkind and rude. The fight wasn't pretty. I saw her sink and I watched hopelessness fill her eyes. I saw the life sucked out of her. I could tell she was thinking, "The same jerk I married is still here. He isn't changing at all."

At that point, I said, "Forgive me. I promise you, I'll spend the rest of my life becoming the man, husband, and father God wants me to be." With that statement, a flicker of hope and life came back to her. I could see it lift her spirits. We continued to grow and develop and, eventually, with small children and a pregnant wife, I moved our family to Oklahoma to attend Rhema Bible Training Center. Following Rhema, we took temporary youth pastor positions at a church in the Midwest as we continued to seek and ask God where He wanted us full time. We heard "Warsaw" in our spirits. We opened a map and found Warsaw, Indiana. We took a day and drove up to the city, and as we did, God gave us a vision of what we were called to do in this community. Without financial backing of any kind, we moved our family to Warsaw, rented a house, rented 25 chairs, put an ad in the paper, and started having services. Over 34 years later (at the time of this writing), we still pastor New Life Christian Church and World Outreach and are so blessed to see what God has done in and through our lives and ministry.

The testimony is powerful and exciting, but I want to point out to you that the entire thing is based on one word: forgiveness. We were one signature away from divorce... **but** *forgiveness*. Forgiveness saved our marriage and continues to save our marriage. Both receiving the forgiveness God gives and releasing it to each other continually through thick and thin. Debbie and I have been able to place a massive gap between ourselves and divorce with this thing called forgiveness. It's a tool that won't just change your life, it will change your *home*.

GOD STANDS ALONE

In 1 Samuel, Samuel heard God, but at first thought it was his earthly father. He equated the voice of God with the authority figure in his life. It's tempting at times, particularly early on in our Christian walk, to compare God to earthly authorities. We can measure God by the leaders we've known, if we aren't careful. That's a mistake, because God truly stands alone. He isn't *in* a separate category. He *is* in a category that is totally separate. Don't view God as you view an earthly father. His mercy and forgiveness exceed that of any earthly figure we've known or seen. Sometimes we are afraid that God is quick to judge and slow to love when the opposite is true. Family can taint us and our perspective, but God wants to clean that up. He doesn't just want to reverse damage that family has done, but He wants to change the family itself.

Joseph so steadily maintained a personal posture of forgiveness. Who were some of the key folks he had to forgive? Family. Those closest to us can sometimes hurt us the most. Why? Because they have the most access to our hearts. There are two true statements about family and forgiveness. We get offended *by* family more than others, *and we* get offended *on behalf of* family more than we get offended for ourselves.

I remember having to attend a funeral, per usual in the ministry life. Personally, I'm extremely mindful of punctuality and absolutely hate being late to anything, especially a funeral in which we are meeting with a fragile family. Debbie was late getting around for it because she had spilled something on herself last minute. I found myself waiting on her.

On the drive to the funeral home, I got quiet, ticked off, and resentful. When we arrived, I shut the car door and left her, quickly walking to the funeral home. She made her way inside after me, and when I was hanging my coat up I said, "When you get around to it, you can join us." I took a mean jab, which was rude and hurtful.

In my eyes, I felt disrespected. I want to be respected and show others respect. Respect is one of the most powerful needs a man has. As a result, I wanted to show respect as much as possible. The reason I was so mad was because I felt like I was being rude and disrespectful to the family by not showing up when I said I would. My wife, on the other hand, felt horrible because she was raised in a house where when she made a mistake, it was a *huge* deal and character assassination. If a silly mistake like spilling something happened, she felt judged and picked apart by family. In the name of jest and fun, the phrase "Debbie's home" was the equivalent of a mess. As a result, when I became irritated with her mistake and made a jab at her, it crushed her and brought back old wounds. Sometimes we don't even realize how far back and how deep words can reach to bring about hurt. I was simply irritated and threw out a jab but did more damage than I had realized. These resolutions and understandings can only be brought about through clear communication and forgiveness.

The next time something like that happened, I came alongside her and said, "It's okay. I'll help you. I'm not mad." This made for a much better outcome! Giving place to anger will forfeit territory of peace to unforgiveness.

"A soft answer turns away wrath, But a harsh word stirs up anger." (Proverbs 15:1)

"If it is possible, as far as it depends on you, live at peace with everyone." (Romans 12:18 NIV)

Review Questions:

How does offense in the home differ from offense outside of it?

_____

_____

_____

_____

_____

_____

_____

_____

_____

In what ways does healthy communication and understanding effect staying free from hurt?

_____

_____

_____

_____

_____

_____

_____

_____

_____

What do your spouse and children feel and experience when you refuse to be hard hearted?

_____

_____

_____

_____

_____

_____

_____

_____

_____

Chapter Nine

The Nuts and Bolts

"It's more practical than you might think..."

Staying mad at *everybody* and *everything* is an impractical way to live. Forgiving not only has practical effects on our lives, but has practical steps to carry it out. I'd like to propose 4 key steps to forgiving offense. It isn't necessarily an all-inclusive list, but it certainly can boost the process!

1) Discover <u>Why</u> The Offense Occurred

Discovering the "why" behind someone's actions can make forgiving so much more manageable. Sometimes, when we discover the "why," the behavior doesn't seem all that wild and off. It causes us to better relate to and understand the situation.

Here's an example. There was an old, old man in a wheelchair and unable to do anything for himself. He was so immobile that his 13-year-old grandson had to feed him and care for him. The job was messy, difficult, and very frustrating. The boy found that at times he was slinging the food and making a mess of it more than he was actually feeding his grandpa. Tired of the messy process and clean up, the boy said to his mom, "I'm done feeding Grandpa. It's so hard to help him. He makes a mess of the food. I'm done."

The frustration was understandable. His mom, however, sat him down and explained the *why*. She said, "Son, have a seat. I want to explain *why* Grandpa is like this. When you were just a baby, an explosion took place in the house. Your dad and I were in the house, and Grandpa happened to be visiting that day. When the explosion happened and the fire starting spreading, we all ran out of the house. I thought that you were in the basement with your dad. Grandpa thought the same thing. Your dad ran out of the house without you because he thought you were with me. We all stopped and looked at each other and realized that none of us had you! With flames enveloping the home, your grandpa ran into the house after you, disregarding the flames, firefighters, and all. He got a wet towel, found you, covered you, and came out with you. During the course of the process, your grandpa sustained severe injuries to his lungs and body. The injuries over time caused him to be unable to talk or move and the effects of the fire limited his muscle movement."

The boy's countenance was certainly changing. She continued, "Grandpa saved your life. In fact, he likes for you to feed him because Grandpa just loves looking at you. When he looks at you, he can see the reason why he paid the price that he paid."

From that day forward, the boy had a 100% different outlook on the frustration of feeding his grandpa. He realized that he was alive because of him and the minor struggle of feeding him couldn't compare to the gratitude he had for rescuing his life. The *why* behind someone's actions can give us a revelation and understanding that makes giving mercy a whole lot easier. If we'll just think and consider the other person's plight, their offensive behavior could make much more sense.

Let me share another story to reinforce this point. There was a man with three very young kids riding the train home. The kids were being disruptive, loud, mean, and simply annoying. They weren't hurting any passengers, they were just sort of in "wild child" mode. They were bouncing off the walls, so to speak. Everyone on the train was growing irritated. Their natural reaction was to do one thing... look at the dad. At that point, they were not annoyed with the kids as much as they were annoyed with the dad who wasn't doing anything. He just sat there with his head in his hands, in some kind of a daze.

Finally, someone walked over and addressed the man. "Okay, bro, when are you gonna deal with the kids? This ride is not pleasant." The dad looked up and said, "I'm sorry. We just came from the hospital. Their mother has just passed away and I don't know how to tell the kids or how to get them to understand." The entire ride shifted from anger to sympathy... from annoyance to sadness. They simply realized the why behind the behavior. If we can understand the reason why the offense has taken place, we will likely find room in our hearts for more grace.

As a closing thought to this point, I will add: knowing the *why* helps the process, but it is not *essential* to the process. You can and should forgive without ever knowing why they did what they did. You might not *ever* have an answer to the "why" question. Whether you do or you don't, forgiveness is a must; however, figuring out the driving motive and situation can certainly make the process easier.

2) Separate the People From the Sin

As a church, there is one thing we must get better at, and that is seeing peoples' value apart from peoples' sin. A person is a person and behavior is behavior. We have to be willing to divide the person from their godless behavior and still choose to see their worth, by faith.

I remember once being in Ukraine in a car on a good long drive. Napping would have been nice, but the driver/host minister wanted to ask me some questions about offense and forgiveness. It was 2am. I splashed water on my face, began sharing, and God's presence came.

I recalled the story of David, Bathsheba, and Nathan to the driver. David should have been out at battle with his fellow men, but instead stayed back. He was out of position, which set him up for failure. While idle on the rooftop, he famously spots Bathsheba bathing and proceeds to commit adultery. Of course, David then sends his faithful soldier and Bathsheba's husband Uriah to the front lines of the war to be slaughtered and killed by the enemy. It was a pathetic act of cowardice and evil.

Following the episode, David got a visit from Nathan the prophet. I call it the story of "Lucky the Lamb." It went as follows.

"Then the Lord sent Nathan to David. And he came to him, and said to him: 'There were two men in one city, one rich and the other poor. The rich man had exceedingly many flocks and herds. But the poor man had nothing, except one little ewe lamb which he had bought and nourished; and it grew up together with him and with his children. It ate of his own food and drank from his own cup and lay in his bosom; and it was like a daughter to him.

"'And a traveler came to the rich man, who refused to take from his own flock and from his own herd to prepare one for the wayfaring man who had come to him; but he took the poor man's lamb and prepared it for the man who had come to him.'

"So David's anger was greatly aroused against the man, and he said to Nathan, 'As the Lord lives, the man who has done this shall surely die! And he shall restore fourfold for the lamb, because he did this thing and because he had no pity.'

Then Nathan said to David, 'You are the man!'" (2 Samuel 12:1-7)

I relayed the story to the driver and was sure to emphasize two points from the story.

A) NOTICE DAVID'S ANGER

David heard the story of the man stealing the lamb and became extremely angry, without knowing that he was the man! When someone is angry about a particular sin, often I wonder what is behind their own life. We tend to get mad about the sin we ourselves struggle with or are guilty of.

B) NEVER JUDGE IN ANGER

I try to never judge a situation in anger. If you notice, David said to Nathan in anger, "As the Lord lives, the man who has done this shall surely die. And he shall restore

fourfold for the lamb…" After he pronounced judgment in anger, Nathan revealed that he was indeed the man. David pronounced judgment on himself. Notice, David said, "He shall restore **fourfold**." If you continue to read the rest of David's life, he tragically lost four children. God didn't have to judge David… he judged himself.

Pronouncing judgment from a place of anger will bring it back on yourself. As I communicated all of these truths, the driver had tears streaming down his face. He said through the interpreter, "Tell Pastor John, I will be more careful now in judging other people." He was deeply touched.

Our temptation is to find ourselves hurt, wounded, offended, and angry, and then pronounce judgment on others when in fact we might just be pronouncing judgment on *ourselves.*

3) Make the Decision

You can't release a hurt without the intentional act of making a quality *decision*. We could talk all day about the ins and outs of forgiveness, why it matters, why we should, and so forth — but it doesn't happen unless a simple decision is made. If forgiveness isn't decisive, it isn't true forgiveness.

It must be a decision in faith, by the Spirit of God, without backing out or finding an alternative. Forgiveness isn't something that we dabble in. It's not something we try out for a few days. It's a commitment. Commitments stick despite inconvenience, feelings, or anything else for that matter.

This decision is not *feelings* based whatsoever. Feelings won't come typically until after the fact. We usually want feelings to influence our decision; the problem is, your feelings will rarely influence you to forgive. It is 100% a faith- and love-based decision.

The Gospel of Matthew spells out an unforgettable parable on forgiveness. "Therefore the kingdom of heaven is like a certain king who wanted to settle accounts with his servants. And when he had begun to settle accounts, one was brought to him who owed him ten thousand talents. But as he was not able to pay, his master commanded that he be sold, with his wife and children and all that he had, and that payment be made. The servant therefore fell down before him, saying, 'Master, have patience with me, and I will pay you all.' Then the master of that servant was moved with compassion, released him, and forgave him the debt.

"But that servant went out and found one of his fellow servants who owed him a hundred denarii; and he laid hands on him and took him by the throat, saying, 'Pay me what you owe!' So his fellow servant fell down at his feet and begged him, saying, 'Have patience with me, and I will pay you all.' And he would not, but went and threw him into prison till he should pay the debt. So when his fellow servants saw what had been done, they were very grieved, and came and told their master all that had been done. Then his master, after he had called him, said to him, 'You wicked servant! I forgave you all that debt because you begged me. Should you not also have had compassion on your fellow servant, just as I had pity on you?' And his master was angry, and delivered him to the torturers until he should pay all that was due to him." Matthew 18:23-34

The master in this story didn't necessarily have goosebumps and lovey feelings for his indebted servant. He didn't examine logic and try to figure out what was best for his organization in terms of finances and loss. Instead, he simply released the servant for the servant's sake. It doesn't have to be feeling-oriented or emotional. The one who based his decisions on feelings was the servant who refused to forgive a tiny debt compared to what he himself had been forgiven.

Feelings can lead you away from forgiveness. Faith and love will bring you back to it. In war, if a man is in a fox hole and a grenade comes rolling in, a soldier doesn't see that grenade as a souvenir. He isn't looking at a relic that he will gladly take home. It isn't exciting. It isn't fun. He sees it as a threat and immediately gets rid of that thing and steers clear of it ASAP. Why? Because it's dangerous! Likewise, we ought to spot unforgiveness when it comes into our territory and immediacy steer clear and throw the thing back to where it came from. It isn't a souvenir or a pet; it's a threat. Forgive quickly and your life will thank you for it.

4) Start Giving

The nature of God is generous. He is a giving God. Forgiven has a root word... "given." Once we have forgiven and released a matter, the giving has only begun. We must adopt a lifestyle of giving.

Giving will keep you ahead of the curb when it comes to bitterness. It'll help reinforce and solidify your decision to let it go. After you have given a situation to the Lord, figure out how you can maximize your generosity and give like crazy!

I know a minister who was saved in a service. They took up an offering, but he had no money and nothing to give. Before the service started, they had given him a pencil and a visitor card. He had nothing so he simply placed the pencil in the offering bucket and ripped a button off of his shirt and placed it in the bucket. It wasn't much, but it was what he had. He began giving *by faith*. Now he operates one of the largest ministries in the entire globe.

A lifestyle of giving will free you from stuff that a stingy person gets stuck on. One of the most profound ways that we can give is through the path of prayer. We not only pay the price in giving but we *pray* the price. Ask God to deeply bless those who have hurt you. Ask Him to seriously put His hand upon them and bless them abundantly. Not only forgiving the offender but praying for the offender helps to seal the deal and it keeps the devil off of your back.

"Neither give place to the devil." (Ephesians 4:27)

Don't pray for God to strike down those who have hurt you. God is not your hitman. When the disciples asked Jesus if they could call down fire from heaven to destroy those who opposed them, Jesus rebuked them in Luke 9:55 and said, "...you do not know what manner of spirit you're of. For the Son of Man did not come to destroy men's lives but to save *them.*" When we pray, we pray for God's best, not God's judgment.

Review Questions:

What about David's life should you try to replicate, and what should you avoid?

_____

_____

_____

_____

_____

_____

_____

_____

Could understanding the "why" behind someone's motives help you process specific things that have been done against you?

_____

_____

_____

When someone prays for a person who has hurt them, what should they ask God to do in their life?

Chapter Ten

Bitterness: The Evangelism Damn

If there is one thing the devil is interested in stealing, it's our witness. We become ineffective in ministering to the world with hard hearts. As believers, if our hearts become angry and bitter, our witness is completely stifled and shut off. We can't afford to allow evangelism to be blocked by bitterness. When you are consumed by a hurt, the last thing on your mind is winning souls. Instead, you are rehearsing what so and so did to you. This is the opposite of the intention of God. The intention of God is for His people to steward their ministry, namely *the ministry of reconciliation.*

"Now all things are of God, who has reconciled us to Himself through Jesus Christ, and has given us the ministry of reconciliation, that is, that God was in Christ reconciling the world to Himself, not imputing their trespasses to them, and has committed to us the word of reconciliation." (2 Corinthians 5:18-19)

God's posture is this: "I worked through Jesus to get people and now I work through people to get other people." What a powerful truth! We can't abandon this call by becoming focused on the shortcomings of others.

Let's look at the life and example of Jesus. His ministry was not bitterly calling out sin. His task wasn't blasting sinners for sin. His task was taking the blast to let sinners become saints.

I remember reading an article about a man whose son was hurt by a next door neighbor. The man put up a literal fence to divide their properties and became extremely embittered. He refused to let the incident go. One day, the Holy Ghost confronted him (as he always does). Not only that, but a charismatic catholic priest pressed him to forgive the incident for 3 months straight.

Finally, he went over to the neighbor's house and knocked on the door. When the neighbor opened it and saw it was him, he covered his face and said, "Don't hit me!" The man simply replied, "I won't hit you. I forgive you."

Three weeks after he went to him and

forgave him, he ran into the man's wife at the grocery store. As they talked, she said that her husband had gotten saved because of the forgiveness he had received from him.

Three weeks after that conversation at the grocery store, he died. The man missed hell because of an act of forgiveness. What could one single choice to forgive mean for your life and the lives of others? Don't allow Satan to steal your ministry of reconciliation through a hardened heart. Stay soft and stay open to the hurting world that God is sending you to.

Review Questions:

Has your witness ever been hindered from a hard heart?

_____

_____

_____

_____

_____

_____

_____

Name some differences in ministry done from a hard heart and ministry done from a soft heart:

_____

_____

_____

_____

_____

_____

_____

In your own words, describe true _reconciliation:_

_____

_____

_____

———————————————————

———————————————————

———————————————————

—————

Chapter Eleven

I Forgive Me

"Come now, and let us reason together,"
Says the Lord, Though your sins are like
scarlet, They shall be as white as snow;
Though they are red like crimson, They
shall be as wool." (Isaiah 1:18)

In the midst of belaboring the subject of forgiveness, it would be a mistake to leave out the value of forgiving one of the most important people you could forgive. There are three administrations of forgiveness in total.

They are as follows:

1)   Forgiveness *from* God.

2)   Forgiveness *to* others.

3)   Forgiveness to *ourselves*.

Giving forgiveness for yourself can be one of the most overlooked but most powerful actions you can take. I know one lady minister who was so self condemned that she would sometimes look in the mirror and just slap herself. Refusing to forgive herself, she would punish herself. Friends, this isn't of God. God desires you to release yourself.

Bitterness toward yourself happens when you become too "performance oriented." You begin to place expectations on yourself that are unrealistic, and as soon as you fail them, you get condemned. It's a recipe for disaster! How can we even begin to forgive others if we still are holding ourselves in a headlock? We must be merciful to ourselves. The problem is, it can seem so counterintuitive to release ourselves when we know what we've done. Love must be a more powerful force than regret in our lives.

SLIPPERS OR SPLINTERS

I know a man who would run around his house as a kid on old wooden floors. His momma always said, "Be sure to always wear your house slippers or else you'll get splinters from these floors!" She was very strict about it and discipline was sure to follow if the kids ran around barefoot.

One day, the boy decided to run and play through the house without slippers, against his momma's warning. He ended up getting a deeply embedded splinter in his foot. He attempted to walk around on it without being noticed. After awhile, it started getting infected. Just lightly pressing his foot to the floor caused serious pain. When he began limping on it, his momma noticed. She asked what was wrong and finally sat him down and looked at his foot. The splinter was massive and infected. He begged her not to pull it out, as he knew the pain would be ridiculous. She yanked that thing out and allowed the healing to begin. Eventually, he was back to normal with a lesson learned. It's funny, so often people are more afraid of the moment of pain that's involved in yanking out the issue than they are a lifetime of continual pain. The boy was fine with walking around in mild pain, but didn't want to experience the moment of extreme pain that would eventually bring healing.

You will cause spiritual infection to set in if you don't forgive yourself and pull out the splinter, so to speak. It might hurt in the moment, but it will bring about total healing in the end. There is no need to ignore a moment of pain to stay in a lifetime of pain. Yank the hurt out and live freely!

It can be challenging conveying these truths. People often don't understand that you're trying to help… instead they think you're trying to cause pain. The boy in that story thought his mom was just causing pain when, in fact, she was bringing about healing. Growing up, I watched my dad work on animals that had wounds. He would often get bit multiple times just positioning the animal to care for its wounds and hurts. Yet the slight pain of the bite was worth the opportunity to care for the animal. Likewise, with people, we run the risk of experiencing a bite when trying to help. Wounded people can lash out. As the saying so often goes, hurting people hurt people.

WHITE AS SNOW

We were once ministering to a young lady

who was about to get married. She was a devout Christian, but slipped up and got pregnant before marriage. We had a meeting with her and the family. In the meeting, her mom blew up and said, "She cannot wear a white dress in her wedding — she is tainted! What do you think, Pastor Lowe?"

I simply said, "The Bible says that Jesus washes our sins as white as snow. She has been forgiven by Jesus and if she wants to, she can wear white." Her mom was simply hurt by the situation and, as a result, she was responding out of that place of pain. At her wedding, she wore white.

Sometimes people around us won't let us forget our mistakes. That makes forgiving ourselves that much more of a mountain to climb. We must choose to value God's intentional Word and His desire for us above such things. In the same way that we forgive others by faith and cling to love, we forgive ourselves and cling to love.

Satan is continually hunting for anything he can get his hands on in your life. If he can get a foothold in your life through self criticism and hatred, he will gladly stick around. Destroy Satan's plans. Remember, forgiveness is an act of violence. Do it.

Review Questions:
Are there places and arenas of your life in which you've condemned yourself?

_____

_____

_____

_____

_____

What are the poisonous effects of not loving yourself?

_____

_____

_____

_____

_____

_____

How do you walk in the balance of loving yourself without being conceited and thinking of yourself too highly?

_____

_____

_____

_____

_____

Closing Thoughts

"Forgiveness is a miracle because in forgiving a man, God imparts to him the power to become the opposite of what he has been." Oswald Chambers

Most of a pastor's time is dealing with people who have self imposed wounds. Forgiveness so often stops the bleeding and closes the wound. Yet, people have to be willing to *give up their right to be hurt.* Hurt comes in all shapes and sizes and in many forms.

We had a good sized family gathering in our home. Family came from out of town. We had a relative who was dating a girl and she came along. When it came time to decide sleeping arrangements, I didn't allow him to share a room with his girlfriend.

Suddenly, I became the bad guy. I refused to allow fornication in my home. I had children I was raising and didn't want them to see that example. The family member and everyone got mad and left. I wasn't popular for the decision.

Charles Spurgeon used to say, "The same sun that melts the wax hardens the clay." The same word, love, and truth that will melt one person might not do the same for another. In fact, some hear it and get ticked, hurt, and hard hearted. My family member certainly belonged to the "hurt and hard hearted" category at first. However, after two months, the family member came under conviction while driving, pulled his car over, cried, and got right with God. He called me and asked me to forgive him and then married the girl. You run the risk of causing offense when sharing truth, but it could also be the saving grace in someone's life.

THE MYSTERY OF OFFENSE

We won't always understand why folks get offended at us. Our job is to simply stay soft and not allow offense to create offense. We had a family in the church who had a house fire. In an effort to help their recovery, we committed to giving a certain sum of money for relief. I gave the check to a man in the church. His job was to deliver it. He went home and put the check on a dresser in his house. In the night, a fan must have been blowing or something and the check fell behind the dresser without him knowing it. As a result, the check never arrived to the family. He simply forgot it. As a result, the lady who suffered a house fire was mad and hated us for three years. All she saw was that we committed to helping and simply didn't. In our eyes, the delivery was made and all was well. We were unaware of the check being lost.

Three years later, the man was moving and found the check and finally took it to her. After the discovery, she called and asked for forgiveness, but never came back to church... (cause that's an awful lot of pride to swallow). Unfortunately, during that three year period, she gossiped and told many people in and around the church that we had committed to helping and didn't keep our promises. Because of a lack of communication, offense came in and caused far too much damage.

FORGIVENESS VS. TRUST

As a closing thought, I wanted to bring out a key truth on this subject matter. I once had a guy lie to me repeatedly and profusely...

which isn't all that uncommon in the ministry. He came clean and asked for forgiveness.

I said to him, "I forgive you, I just don't trust you." When you tell people, "I forgive you, but I don't trust you," they freak out. I calmly reminded the man, "You just lied to me repeatedly." He responded, "Yeah, but you're a Christian!" I said, "Yes. And forgiveness is extended and given freely, but trust is earned."

In the midst of learning about the practical and spiritual applications of forgiveness, let's not forget that forgiveness and trust are not equivalents. Just because you forgive doesn't mean that you trust. You can be completely free from a person's offense and hurt without jumping right back into the mess and trusting them. We must keep our hearts soft and clean in terms of forgiveness while using wisdom in where we place our trust.

Furthermore, just because someone is forgiven doesn't mean that they escape legal consequences of certain actions here on earth. Many people make the mistake of thinking that because their record is cleared in the sight of God their record should be cleared in the court systems. We still have natural consequences to bear sometimes, yet God gives assistance through it all!

Forgiveness isn't optional. It isn't a "potential route" for a believer. It's an absolute must. It's a non-negotiable. It's life and death and can only be achieved by and through the love of the Father, the grace of the Son, and the power of the Holy Spirit.

ABOUT THE AUTHOR

Pastor John B. Lowe II has been faithful in the full time ministry for over 34 years. He carries a heart for the local church in Warsaw, yet has reached a world wide audience, ministering in many nations of the world, leading pastors conferences, marriage conferences, faith meetings, and more. Pastor and his lovely wife, Debbie, have four children and three daughter-in-laws who all serve God; John Bryan & Alyssa Lowe, Jeremiah & Lauren Lowe, Michael and Alisha Lowe and Brightie Lowe. They also have six beautiful grandchildren; John Bradyn, Nevaeh, Kyra, Aubrey, Noah and Zaya.

Made in the USA
Columbia, SC
15 March 2018